Rise

> **"THE KEY IS TO RISE,
> NO MATTER WHAT HAPPENS.
> ALWAYS RISE.
> JUST LIKE IN LIFE."**

I HEARD MYSELF SAY THOSE WORDS WHILE COACHING,
AND THEY SOUNDED DUMB YET SOMEHOW RIGHT.

ALWAYS RISE.

SO STUPID, AND YET SO SIMPLE. AND, REALLY, THE KEY TO
EVERYTHING. CHEST UP. EYES STRAIGHT AHEAD. HOLD YOUR
BREATH. GO DEEP INTO THE HOLE AND ... RISE.

I COULD WRITE A MILLION WORDS, BUT NONE COULD MAKE
THE MESSAGE ANY CLEARER FOR YOUR SQUAT AND YOUR LIFE.

YOU ONLY NEED ONE WORD TODAY, AND ALL THESE DAYS:
RISE

RESIST THE URGE
TO CONSUME THIS BOOK RAPIDLY.

YOU MIGHT WANT TO GULP AND RUSH AND READ ALL THE PAGES AS QUICKLY AS POSSIBLE.

FIGHT THAT IMPULSE.
MASTER YOUR URGE.

THIS IS A BOOK TO SAVOR, TO RUMINATE UPON, TO HOLD AND PONDER.

GO ONE THOUGHT AT A TIME. JUST ONE.

YOU CAN START ANYWHERE. JUMP AROUND, OR GO IN ORDER. IT'S ALL UP TO YOU. BUT DON'T GULP. TAKE ONE SIP. READ A PAGE (OR TWO). THINK. PUSH THAT THOUGHT AROUND IN YOUR HEAD ALL DAY. AT WORK, IN THE GYM, AT HOME. HOW DOES THIS THOUGHT APPLY TO ALL THREE PLACES? TO YOUR LIFE? OR DOES IT APPLY?

TOMORROW, WAKE UP AND PICK ANOTHER THOUGHT FOLLOW THE SAME ROUTINE. LINGER ON THAT THOUGHT ALL DAY.

GO SLOW, TAKE YOUR TIME, BE THE BEST LOVER OF THESE WORDS. PICK THEM UP, WORK WITH THEM, FEEL THEIR RESPONSE. NOTICE THE WAY THE WORDS LAY ON THE PAGE. SINK INTO THEM. BE.

IF YOU DO IT THIS WAY, YOU WILL GUARANTEE YOURSELF A GLORIOUS, DELICIOUS, EXHILARATING MONTH OR TWO.

BEGIN. AND ENJOY.
LISBETH

Start.

You will grow stronger on the journey, not by waiting for it to begin.

Believe you are worthy of magnificence. "

Move your feet
and everything changes.

When you feel scared and lost,
remember this:

KICK ASS ◇ MOVE ◦ THINK ◦ DO ◇ BELIEVE ◦

We all are.

"The weight will feel as light as you think it is."

"  **"**

Rise. Always rise.

"Get in the habit of surprising yourself.

Surprise yourself at least once a day.

More, if you would achieve. "

Better, not perfect.

_____

(Aim for perfect but be at peace
if you fall short.)

Fill your life with people who have light in their eyes.

" Don't Do Let

be afraid.
your work.
life happen.

99

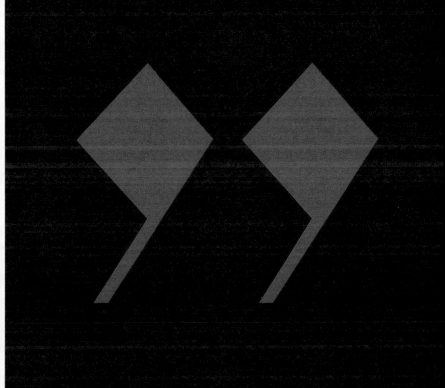

"You can this day."

handle

> **There's nothing sexier than being who you are.**

‹ START ◇ SEE ⦂ GROW ‹ LOVE ◇ PERSEVERE ⦂

You may ask yourself: Who am I to be audacious? "

Ask yourself instead: Who are you not to be?

"Make the effort, or own the regret."

"Movement

is life,

but it does not

have to become

your entire life.

Get your head right or go home,

"

Princess.

"Barbells, books, love: not everything in life, but close. Damn close."

"Part of strength is determining when to use your strength."

If I said,

"You are beautiful" would you believe me?

—

"

Don't wait forever. That's boring.

"

"Let go of what is not working for you."

—

"Do what you have to do, and more. So much more."

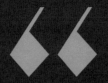

Keep going.

Be scared, be unsure.

That's okay.

But don't

be stopped.

Half of weightlifting is quieting your "

mind.
"

It is crucial to remember that the process

is where

we get
stronger
and
better.

You are not yet who you will be, but neither are you who you were.

"

This is progress and victory, if you choose to see it that way.

Well, you can't lift it

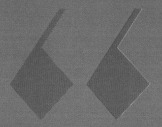

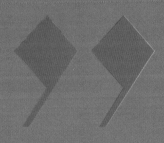

TODAY.

Look down at your barbell.

Look up at the sky.

Which is bigger?

The thing you're scared to say

is sometimes exactly what might set you free.

" You determine your self=worth. You determine your story.

Not memory or anybody else. You. 🥂

You keep you from being free.

Letting go

of what is

not working

is almost

as important

as perseverance.

The heart will grow stronger only if you test it

— in the gym and in love.

You absolutely

do not suck

as much as you

think you do.

"
If you're only focusing on the future, you are missing life right now. "

Throw

down

when

you

must

The unfortunate reality is that no one can truly show you the way. You're going to have to find it for

yourself. 99

Life is movement:

—————— mental,

—————— physical,

—————— spiritual.

Perhaps all three,
if you're lucky
and determined.

The barbell has no usefulness until you pick it up.

" "

"

Nobody gets stronger

by staying the same.

"

Joy is resilience.

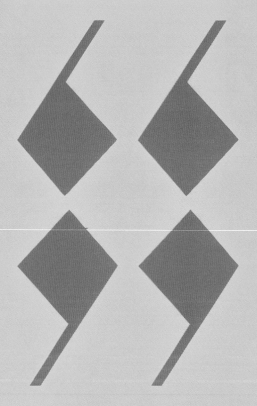

Joy is the biggest weapon we have. Joy can be the ultimate "Fuck you."

"

If you think the barbell

is the most important

thing in this life, then you

might need a quick hard

slap across the face.

"

"Think of all the fun you could have if you didn't take yourself so seriously. "

You

can

prepare forever,

but

eventually

it comes down

to you and the

weight on you.

Pull the stopper off your tongue.

Rip the guard from your ego. Go for it all.

"

That which diminishes you is not making you stronger.

"

Who told you that you weren't as good as the others?

And why did you

believe them?

Fear not your own strength. You have it for a reason. Use it.

A strong mind

and

a strong body

is not a combo

to fuck with.

When they tell you

that you're

too old,

or too young,

or too inexperienced,

you tell them you're

not dead.

And then

keep going.

Look at that.

Wow.

Lift it.

Yes, the bar is heavy.

Stop thinking.

I can.

Wait.

Lift it?

I can't.

I can't do this.

The bar is so heavy.

I'm not strong enough.

I couldn't ever lift it.

(now read it in reverse order)

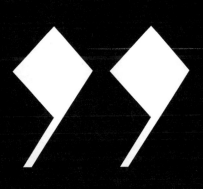
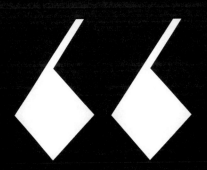

Rise

Made in the USA
Lexington, KY
06 February 2016